Here Go the Knives

Here Go the Knives

poems & illustrations
by Kelsey Bryan-Zwick

MOON
TIDE PRESS

~ 2022 ~

Here Go the Knives

© Copyright 2022 Kelsey Bryan-Zwick

Editor-in-chief
Eric Morago

Editor Emeritus
Michael Miller

Marketing Specialist
Ellen Webre

Proofreaders
Jim Hoggatt & Ellen Webre

Front cover art
Kelsey Bryan-Zwick

Author photo
Donna Hilbert

Book design
Michael Wada

Moon Tide logo design
Abraham Gomez

Here Go the Knives
is published by Moon Tide Press

Moon Tide Press
6709 Washington Ave. #9297
Whittier, CA 90608
www.moontidepress.com

FIRST EDITION

Printed in the United States of America

ISBN # 978-1-957799-00-1

Dear Reader,

These are the poems that make me feel human, though they may indeed make you feel strange. My hope is that for some—my fellow spoonlings, painlings, and scolio-siblings, those whose diagnosis took a wrong turn, who struggled to be heard and believed and acknowledged—these poems will feel like home. Like a mirror, like recognition, portraits from our world behind the hospital curtain.

Not that pain is singular. Not that it is universal. Not that it is unique. Perhaps just a box of paradoxes to open upon a dare. But pain happens. Everyday. Like breathing. Maybe to you or to someone you love. Perhaps a stranger. Someone draws the short straw. I drew the squiggly one with lots of kinks in it.

And this is that story. A story about pain. About survival. A story about an American life. My disabled American life.

So, I dare you to read it. To flip through the pages. To accept fate, because *Here Go the Knives.*

Yours,
KB-Z

Contents

Scoliosis   13

III of Swords

The Cut   17
Idiopathic Curvature   18
Girl with Scoliosis Plays Soccer   19
Admission   20
Scrambled Eggs   21
Our Tradition   22
Senbazuru   23

Strength VIII

Letter to Ansel   27
Body of Art   28
(Mad)woman in the Attic/Invisible Stones   30
Forgetting the Flowers   31
The Image Mirages Once Upon Waking Up   32
Kintsugi   34
X-Rays, MRIs, CTs, Bone Scans   35
Just Discovered   36

IX of Swords

Sister   39
I Draw the Nine of Swords   40
Under the Bone Saw   41
Poem in VII Parts   43
Corset 2.0   45
Not a Nightmare   47
I Drop the Knives   48
Sometimes the Knives   49

X of Swords

Waking Up in Hospital   53
Agoraphobia   54
The ransom notes   55
Anatomy of Noise   56
Speaking Ill   57
My Skeleton   59
Self-portrait   61
Pain, Capital P   62

IV of Swords

The Way Willful Neglect Burns
   Through Like California Wildfire   65
Overlapping Venn Diagrams   66
Nothing but the Bells   67
The River of Styx and Stones   68
Hand-Me-Downs   69
How I Hide   70
Yolk: Albumen: Shell   72
The light that shines through   73
Making Space: Small Pieces I Feed the Earth   74

The High Priestess

Experimental Fairytale   77
Clutched in My Fist the Bag I Carry   79
The Magician's Assistant   80
There is no Time to Learn French   81
Music   83
Peaches Three Ways   84
Love Doesn't Always Glimmer Like a Horse   85
Your Mouth Is a Cutting Board—Mine Is a Knife   86
New Love   88

X of Wands

Of Poems & Folded Promises   91
Wearing an Armband with my Name, Date of Birth,   92
and Scannable Barcode   92
We're Not Quite Friends   93
My Feet Thwackadoodle   95
Left Thigh   97
To Describe this Body I Invent   98
Poem Without a Name   99
Gravity   101
Letter to My Forgetful Self   102
Vulture,   103

Knight of Swords

Rate Your Pain   107
In My Nearly Nine Years Applying   109
for Disability Recognition   109
The Old Man's Boss Isn't the Boss's Old Man   110
We Smile   112
Cause and Effect   114
modern robot   115
The Prize   117

Queen of Swords

If a Poem Was a Dress   121
Sitting in the Coffeeshop   122
Quartet   123
The KB-Z Operating Manual   124
My Name   125
On the Other Side of the Blade   127
Pressed Flowers   128
Body Love   129
This Body   130
For Unknown   131
Setting the Curve   133
Pebble and Tide   134
Occasionally Pink, or White   135
For the Love of What is Holy   136

About the Author   *139*
Acknowledgements   *140*

Every man has a right to live
Love is all that we have to give

— Jimmy Cliff

Imagination is better than a sharp instrument.
To pay attention, this is our endless and proper work.

— Mary Oliver

Scoliosis

Unplugging the bathtub drain with my curved toes,
numb, where I cannot bend to reach, learning this and
to have self-esteem, even with legs unshaved, toenails
grown long, hair unwashed, wound crusting over, blood
in my mouth from intubation, back of the throat scratch
letting the cup half-full, fall and shatter with stunted reflex,
letting someone else to tidy the jagged edges—as I contend
with mending my own, placing the odds on myself, even
as the doctors explain the risks, explain the need—to once
again sharpen their knives.

III of Swords

The Cut

The first time I went under the knife
I was eleven
my parents asked their friends and co-workers
to donate blood
which they did
they also gave me a basket of get-well gifts

My best friends gave me a teddy bear
and a Goo-Goo Dolls CD
My soccer coach's daughter gave me a CD player
and headphones

After the surgery
which went rougher than expected
I laid in bed for two months
with someone else's blood in my veins
watching the leaves outside my window move
listening to the music in my headphones
hugging the bear tight

Idiopathic Curvature

Without cause, or known reason,
no antidote, no cure, no vaccine for
gravity itself defined exists here
without rhyme or care for an exit.

      Twelve separate bones
      must become one—
      a shock, a suspension
      cut, must absorb all
      this feeling in my guts.

It takes most of the day for the doctors
to straighten my spine as much as the rest
of my body will allow.

The longer I am laid out on the operating
table, the more my opened skin begins to dry
out, the scar forming before I am stitched.

      When I wake up, I am
      two inches taller than
      when I got to the hospital,
      only I don't know it yet—
      I can't get out of bed.

Girl with Scoliosis Plays Soccer

She sweats like other children do,
runs after the ball, gives chase with them.
Grass stains her knees as she slides
her body between cleat and ball.
Before the ball can be shot at the goal,
she pushes it with the force of her slide
out of bounds. We see her—mud smeared
on jersey, ponytail pulled tight—rise up.
She sees her future, the need to grab handrail.
Unsteady, before ground crashes in,
to curl and tumble as she slips and falls.
The need to train muscle and reflex, she is
willing her body, willing to break skin
to bruise, and bleed. She is not keeping score.
She never cares if she wins. More than just fun,
like a dancer, she is learning the moves—
how to tackle the ground with grace, how
to think as the ball as the world speeds
towards open face. She sees this.
She runs forward, head first.

Admission

Standing against the light of entryway,
the nurse says, *It's for the vampires*
downstairs in the basement,
after I ask, for the umpteenth time,
why they have to keep drawing blood.

It's 2 a.m. and the blood pressure machine
makes my arm go limp the way it
squeezes and I know she's right,
cuz I'm eleven and know more about vampires

than I can process the outcome
of another anemia test, the three pints
waiting for me in the freezer, the oxygen
itchy in my chapped nostrils,
and the little red-polka dot
pin-point needle marks.

I'm that thirsty now.
Could drink it down.
Full and warm
like hot cocoa.

Scrambled Eggs

The commercial circa the 90s, you may
remember, smashes the whole egg
with a frying pan. Says, *This is your brain
on drugs!* The dripping mess of it all over
the kitchen and I am freaked out—freaking
out—all eleven years of me and post-op
my poor brain, I think, *how it will suffer*
as I swallow the pills the doctors prescribe,
remember the morphine drip, but with
such a smashed-up brain I begin to wonder
if what I am remembering is at all true.
My cracked shell, my oozing.

Our Tradition

Whatever the scans say, we wait, my mother and I
in line to get our hot fudge sundaes from McDonald's—
the only restaurant at the LA Children's Hospital
except for the cafeteria which brings forth too many
memories, for either of us to eat there willingly again.

It's our treat after a day, after years of x-rays, and being
in waiting rooms with all the other bent-up ortho kids
in our various degrees of casting, frames, and immobility—
we begin to laugh at the absurdity of it, that after all this
worry, the doctors don't appear to mind if our only nutritional
choice really is the greasy sweet of fast food.

Consumed with the repetition of concerned updates, difficult
decisions, troublesome looks, and paused reassurances,
we need to laugh—as my mother and I hold on to each
other, to our delicious and dripping plastic cups, licking
spoons on the way home, the long drive, sitting in traffic
sometimes a quiet between us, sometimes crying.

Senbazuru

Maybe I should have read up on the tradition better,
but when I got diagnosed and Sadako's story was first shared with me,
what I understood was that if I folded my thousand paper cranes, a wish
would be granted. And so, I made them as a young girl might, from waxy
bubble gum papers, tinfoil peeled carefully back from chocolate bites,
from napkins at restaurants, and from the corners of homework sheets.
Starburst wrappers were a particular favorite—though I didn't like
the chewy sweets inside and would feed them to a best friend.
And at the greyhound station, children would bring me their dollars
to fold, each of us, sharing now our fate. Like so many autumn leaves,
I left and gave and nudged my birds into the winds, let these children,
let each stranger, find a bit of luck.

Strength VIII

Letter to Ansel

It is your photos I tape to the walls
along the hallway where I walk with hobbled
step, toward an imagined ridge—see myself not
here stuck at home for yet another month
of the year, another year of my life, elsewhere
instead, among the tall pines of Yellowstone
staring down the granite faces of Yosemite,
I swear I look across your vistas as I trudge,
willing one foot after the next through fallen
sycamore leaves, to the bed, to the kitchen sink
where the cold waters of Mirror Lake swirl,
how I let myself go in and into your beauty
when I cannot know my own.

Body of Art

1. I awake as a Picasso painting
    a nude from his Cubist period
    jumbled, an ill-fitting jigsaw
    pelvic hip has been chiseled
    pressed into spinal column
    my face puffed and itchy
    the opiates have me confused
    with somebody else

2. I awake as one of Salvador Dali's
    melted clocks, there is something
    besides time passing here, my body
    blobbish, must be folded into plaster
    to make torso cast, the metal has had
    to be removed, the scoliosis still un-
    fused, the drainage tubes where I seep
    from me, I can't help it, and Scream
    like all Edvard Munch styled

3. I awake as Frida Kahlo's self-portrait
    my broken back, her broken back
    the dream seems to become more real
    tugs at the peripherals, images
    superimposed, a pattern shapes motif
    a picture of life, stills, comes into focus

4. I awake as a Grecian statue
    ancient busted-bust, the shoulder
    blade, ribs, left thigh, have gone
    numb, covered in dust, in the rubble
    sheets draped like a toga
    I eat my grape Jell-O, adjust
    the bed, recline towards relief

5.   I awake as the Bride of Frankenstein's
Monster's Doppelgänger, the screws
in my neck tighten as the clouds are
about to gather, my movements
static, wires connected to me beep
in the electric machine, my eyes turn
green when lightning strikes

6.   I awake as the Bionic Woman
or the cost of pale and sickly
has me looking like a million bucks
and really this is my fortune
to experience art as canvas or
great slab of stone, to be sculpted
scalpeled, painted with iodine
combined with rare metals, gilded
this body worth its weight and
worthwhile, gold and golden

(Mad)woman in the Attic/Invisible Stones
For Bertha Rochester, Née Mason

I too have been put away
all of us eating from our meager cups
of watery truth, dousing ourselves
in a blessing of less.

I remember in class when I first read
Jane Eyre, not even one hand went up
to question why you'd been locked away
chained, not even mine.

What madness to let you loose, to dare
to love you, just as you were, who would
care for the invisible stone in their shoe?
Only a rose loves its thorns.

What could have saved you was
taken away, not a penny for you
to claim, no way to break free
only you were left. A hero rose

to ashes, you burned down the house
that wouldn't let you go, that torch
I carry into a field of attics, future
unknown.

Forgetting the Flowers
For Greta Thunberg

The way a moth flies into the flame
gray wings singed to the hot glass
of light bulb

The way a man crawls over the railing
of a bridge he knows other men
have jumped off

The way a child circles a crayon inside
and outside, then inside the lines again
trying to draw a world in which we don't
get so turned around anymore

The Image Mirages Once Upon Waking Up

shimmers just so as I lie in my blue backless gown—
recuperating from the deep sleep that exists in this place without dreams—
as a woman, another patient, is wheeled into the predischarge area.
All of us are hooked up to *beeping* monitors with our IV's
plugged in, and the steady rhythm of mechanical inflating
blood pressure machines, recording this odd song.

Muffled noises coming from behind the pulled privacy curtain,
two beds over, I hear the nurse flustering over the woman, over the body
of the woman. On repeat the nurse is insisting, *Relax, you need to
relax.* Commanding on a loop, *Relax your arm. You need to
relax your arm.* The tension is ever increasing in her tone, *Re-lax!
You need to relax!* And with each iteration I feel my own tensions rise.

Having been anesthetized time and time again, having found
my own way out of the complete blankness, under a blanket
of confusion, I imagine hearing this stranger first thing, their alarm call
of a voice, orders, uncompassionate to one's bewilderment,
as the trauma of the experience surfaces (the needles, the knives),
trying to grasp at comprehension—I think I might find my fists
balling up, ready for a fight.

Just as the nurse barks again, without synonym or variation,
Relax! Except in sharpness, *You Need To Relax! Relax! Your! Arm!*
Exasperated as I chime in, *Well maybe if you would stop yelling, she might
be able to.* Audible enough for another nearby nurse to shuffle on
to the scene, when in a voice like fresh water, I hear them with soft inquiry
ask, *Can you understand me?* Gently, *Do you know where you are?*
With reassurance, *You're in the hospital, just waking up
after your procedure.*

And I relax. Knowing someday—maybe sooner than even
I would like—I'll be that woman. That woman will be me.
Ten minutes later and I tune back in, she is speaking calmly now
both woman and nurse. Nobody knows exactly what
happened, like the conversation I heard as they wheeled me
into the operating room, words I swore I'd write down—how now
I don't remember a line of it. How the woman won't remember
this, how that nurse just might, how maybe behind the pulled curtain
lying in my blue backless gown, I can't really be sure that any of this
even happened at all.

Kintsugi
The art of repairing pottery with gold

I offer my broken body, time and time again
upon the operating table, as rapid hands shine
they pour in rare metals, trying to keep me whole
enough to hold my own water, my own blood.

X-Rays, MRIs, CTs, Bone Scans

Going through my EOBs
and all I can think about
is how I've been lit up
like a Christmas tree, like a
small town, the way the night
sky used to be, and that maybe
soon I'll be glowing, glow
in the dark, or electric to
the touch, with or without
contrast, and radioactive
isotope injections, so, I try
to stay cool, and emanate
all that I am.

Just Discovered

I am the lean in the tilt
all curves on curves
twin outward spirals coiling
nautilus shell rounds

I am organic amoeba
rough sketched pantomime
spin art chrysalis in neon
colors, glow in the dark
stars, backlit bioluminescent
rhapsody blues

I am the crunch of ponderosa
pine, rosemary, yarrow, wild
mint, the suave of plumeria
on the breeze, the overblown
palm frond left roadside
like the unnamed flower, I am
just discovered

IX of Swords

Sister

Sometimes I stick things in a drawer
not thinking, because I found my sister
in a drawer, after she died—every paperclip,
every mismatched earing, held her, her
last gifts to me, and I do not want to be
a dead thing, but I want to be found.

Needed past giving—so that every remnant
becomes sacred artifact, becomes a whisper
of the truth—her voice, I miss her voice.

I Draw the Nine of Swords

Cripple, disabled retard
Handicappedlame

They all sounded like slurs to me
Growing up trying to hide myself
From myself

Sounded bad like something
I didn't want to be
Who chooses pain and suffering
Who yelps and who bleeds

I wring the night like a towel
I towel my fear like a grip
I grip the white knuckles of my
Punching bag soul

I kick and I scream
But only on mute
Only off camera
Backstage
Behind the curtain

I cry into the cups of my hands
Gimp, hobbled horse, ill
My fate
My fate
My fate
I weep

Under the Bone Saw

This mark here, made up of seven scars now
or   rather
where one scar was cut open and removed
then replaced with fresh wound crusting over.
Removed so that the web of rippled smooths
does not keep extending as gnarled knots
throughout my ever-increasingly mangled body
but gone too—any and all memories these scars
harbored of renewal.

And then a third   and then a fourth
and then a fifth layer excavated, exposed
and I, the body chalk outline in this experience
remain unburied, forming new and newer skin.

A seventh layer reached, inner anthropology
erased, empty pages examining themselves,
unmapped nakedness revealed to my inner palm.

Before my scar, my spine was so bent up in double
curve that I grew inches on the operating table
as I was unfurled like a leaf.

So fast that one of my lungs nearly collapsed
pop
made stretch marks of my hips, freed somehow
from the rest of me.

The second time though, I very nearly died—
I mean they made soup of my insides,
or rather the metal Harrington rods and hooks
supporting my reconfigured bones   did.

Allergic.

Removed with saw,
they had to put in extra drains, but even after
they sewed me up I kept on leaking
through the torso cast, each scar
fault lines reshaping somehow
each scar m/in/e.

Poem in VII Parts

I.
my stack of doctor's business cards is growing
a deck I shuffle like appointments throughout the week
like weeks throughout the year

I flip to see which oracle's x-ray vision will cast its sight
upon my haggard demons, my boney-dense skeleton
which blood magic practitioner will require the minerals in my veins
which scryer demand coin to search for my freshwater well of being

today the card says drive an hour north,
sacrifice vitals to the afternoon winter sun
take the given supplement to quiet the hum of beehive in inner ear

II.
shuffle the deck
Hermit predicts
a day at home with the cats
12 long naps
longer than life
I dream

III.
like Pluto and planet X
my sister and I orbit each other
two misnamed comments
at the edge of the galaxy
dancing in and out of known
life

IV.
I Ouija with the cats
call fourth animal spirits
to comfort me alone in the machine
naked on the table

V.
I blow out the candle I lit to ward off bad luck. I pluck the chimes like the wind. I ring a bell to the next world. I knock on the wood to prevent a jynx. I spit for spilt salt. I weep for wasted milk. I take the cheese as far as it will go. I dumpster dive to feed myself through college. I watch as they scatter my sister's ashes into the Pacific Ocean. Two sea lions play below wooden Santa Cruz pier, the rollercoaster is running at the board walk where the mechanic-psychic tells me:

VI.
we hold hands
and the lines of your palm
read the lines of my palm
we invent our own handshake
and make a deal
to keep chasing sunsets

VII.
a new shuffle of papers arrives
I read close to the page
how to wash my body and when
the clothes required, items to avoid
no makeup, no polish, no lotion, no underwear
remove shoes and glasses
revert into soft animal underparts
and blurred vision, place all your
personal belongings within lockbox
wait here   drink this   provide a urine sample
tell them where it is tender   what you ate
for your last meal, the last time
you drank any water   can you feel your feet?
wiggle your toes   follow my pen with
only your eyes?

Corset 2.0

The torso-cast I wear
has teeth
eats my bedsheets
tears the clothes
I wear
with the metal teeth
clasps and gnashes

I synch the corset,
of Madonna's inverted shape:
hard-white plastic form
with the boobs cut out,
around my twelve-year-old
adolescence

This cast: snapshot in time
my breathing encased
in plaster mold, my collapsed
lungs rearranging
inner space
within imprint made
upon waking from
emergency surgery

All the metal they had to
hack away from my spine
and bits of muscle and bone
an empty space squishing
as they roll me away from
my pound
of scar tissue, which they test
for cancers, infections
to find rare metal allergy

the reason, all of a sudden clear—
why my pierced ears itch and scab
why my braced teeth flame up
why I am laid open for a second time

The torso cast has teeth
speaks to me in riddles
with synched clasps,
a mouth that reveals
without wanting to
a mouth I shed only
once a day

my mush of skin released
for one hour a night
pool of soapy bath, my only naked
hour of solace, where I watch
the disheveled cast,
from the warm hub of bathwater

disassembled
on the bathroom floor
teeth loose in their mouth
smiling up at me

Not a Nightmare

I fall asleep dreaming
of being stabbed repeatedly
by butcher knives. And
I know now that I need
yet another surgery when
I wake up happy, rested.

I Drop the Knives

I drop the knives
when I try to chop vegetables
or when I want to cut
your sandwiches in half

I drop the knives, knock them
over, like cups and plates break
and I find little bits of glass
with the pads of my feet

I drop the knives
when the dog loudly barks
I drop the knives
when I wheelchair the awkward
angles of our studio apartment
the narrow of our small kitchen

I drop the knives
but keep missing my feet
though as the numbness
grows up the trellis of my legs

I drop the knives
and wonder if I'll feel the blade
or just bleed, like how sometimes
I only know there is glass
in my foot by the trail
of little red dots across the floor

Sometimes the Knives

sometimes the knives cut peaches, sometimes
the knives cut bread, sometimes they cut pink
or sideways, an onion, a thumb, sometimes
the knives cut the doorway that lets you in

sometimes the knives cut promises, sometimes
the knives cut skin, sometimes you can feel the knives
sometimes you can't feel anything at all, sometimes
the knives are unspoken, sometimes they shout
sometimes your friends jump in to break up the fight
sometimes the knives are your friend, your only friend
sometimes the knives are a tool, sometimes you are

sometimes the knives make you feel brave,
sometimes the knives are a warm gun, sometimes
the knives are a cold wound, sometimes the knives
grow larger at the thought as if stuck in a bad dream,
sometimes the knives shrink, like they drank a swift
potion, sometimes the knives forget, sometimes
the knives sink in just as you realize *why it's all*
so beautiful in the first place, sometimes you think
well, shit

sometimes the knives are a murder of crows holding
symposium, a bad omen in the back of the throat,
sometimes salvation, sometimes the moon, sometimes
the knives are a tarot card overturned, salt spilt on the table
spit, circle, circle, dot, dot, now you got the cootie shot
to the arm, sometimes the knives are stuck in your back
sometimes held to your jugular, sometimes the knives are
free-falling, myriad as rain drops, and you have to catch
them with your bare hands, sometimes you are the knives

sometimes you are the knives and you have to cut
and cut and cut until you can see your way through again
even when you can't imagine what is on the other side
you know you can't live like this, sometimes you trade
the knives for hot soup, a warm place to sleep, sometimes
the knives get lost in the mail, lost as you are, sometimes
the knives are a spoon and you dig, sometimes it is into
the ground, sometimes it's out, covered in earth, sometimes
the knives are cleaned this way, sometimes the knives
disappear or bend, with only the power of an idea

sometimes you cut before you think, sometimes
you wretch at the thought, sometimes the knives
are a stranger, sometimes the knives are an aunt,
sometimes the knives are in the drawer, sometimes
in the butcher's block, sometimes right at hand
sometimes just out of reach, sometimes the knives
spread the butter, sometimes it is vegan butter,
sometimes the knives mix paint, sometimes it is
red paint, sometimes the knives are made of paper,
sometimes the knives are a bloodless moon, sometimes
the knives

sometimes the knives won't stop and you have to decide
you won't either, that your teeth are sharper, that
you'll use anything and everything you have to survive,
sometimes in the hole you dug you plant a garden,
sometimes you bury your dead, sometimes you leave
your mark so you remember everything you've been,
sometimes you hide your treasure, why you had to use
the knives at all, sometimes the knives are the nest egg
that let you retire, sometimes you die with the knives
hidden under your tongue, sometimes the knives are the words
you write and write and

sometimes the knives remove a tiny splinter
from the bottom of a tiger's paw, causing so much pain
you hold the knives as you hold the soft fur of the tiger's leg,
sometimes the knives are forgiveness, sometimes you say
you say, *here go the knives*, and you give them your bleeding
heart, your exposed breast, your ready stance, your best
yoga-warrior pose, your smile, you give your knives
sometimes you give your best knives, your only knives
however you can

X of Swords

Waking Up in Hospital

The message—heavy clocks
    that hang from the grey—washed walls
        are wired to you, monitoring rhythms,

        promise that you are not yet preserves in formaldehyde.

The music sounds like bombed—
    out roads, only a few wing bones
        left, mangled, the way sparrows
            begin their anxious coo-cooing and repeat.

Who listens to birds any-hoos?

        Officially the procedure is called
          Rainbow Disassembling, some antiquated
            mother's milk to be fed to spine.

How many ambiguities
    switchblade through the night shift
        as I lie wild beauty of a mess?

        Wound hot and itchy with reforming.

My mind is a three-piece suit, letter-pressed
    I vomit, weep, scream, quiet flutes

        in the dark, whole body becomes outlined
            in feeling—evidence of a tomorrow.

Agoraphobia

Forgetting how to leave the home
to spend all the spoons it takes
to mouth past the cats, to dress
to hello and awkward lip small talk
with friends that know you but also
know how nervous you can get
just trying to get through one sentence
without the word *surgery*.

The ransom notes

come disguised as medical bills
gagging my wages, binding me with debt,
my own body held hostage from itself
health at the far end of the river I am
trying to navigate; the ferryman waits
as I pluck the coins from my eyes.

Anatomy of Noise

Despite our many walls and fences, closed doors
and shut-up windows, the noise outside, inside
invades—jerks, jolts, beeps, screeches, knocks
street sweepers, car alarms, and engine revs.

The noise outside barks incessantly, likewise jets
test and sonic booms the whole neighborhood,
shrouded in low flying airplanes, the bus honks
lawn mower always mowing someone else's lawn.

Underneath is a constant hum and haw and drill
and droll of things, the refrigerator plugged in,
the heater buzzing in the vents, the computer fan,
clock ticking, lights on and off in florescent overheads.

A chorus of uncoordinated din, distorting the world
electric, and maybe I wouldn't mind so much except
for all these lingering memories I don't have—surgical
power tools, eerie phantom pitch echoing of hollowing out
bone, turning screws, the bolts—unremembered trauma,
sharping the noise like knives.

Speaking Ill

Sometimes, mid-sentence even, I stop
a breath short from mentioning my sister
who died.

Because in the awkward paused space
someone eventually tries to fill this silence
with a condolence, *Deepest sympathies,*
with the question:

How did she die?

And I don't want to lie, I want to scream
I don't want to say. Like the rest of us
one day, she stopped breathing.

Breathing. That's all she could do
near the end. And that was only with
the help of machines.

I don't want to say we had to decide
one day to unplug those machines, to stop
the pumps keeping her alive.

I don't want to say
I want to scream—
the words fall from
my face like stones.
Cirrhosis of the liver.

She had some health problems
those final few years she was always
in and out of the emergency room.

I didn't go to visit
that last time in the hospital,
before leaving to go back to school.
It felt like suffocating, sitting there
watching her wounds.

Alcoholism mostly. There had been
a bad weight loss surgery that changed
how her liver processed things, or didn't,
but she knew she had to stop drinking
and she couldn't. Didn't. Though it was
a little sip—*Only little slips*—she'd insist.
Just one celebratory glass of wine.

I don't want to say how I had to clean
out her room, the stashes and stashes
of pills I found, prescribed bottles
I threw out one by one with bare and
grieving hands.

I don't want to say. I want to scream
I don't want you to think it was her fault
she was so sick, not even the doctors could
cure her.

My Skeleton

She sits sipping tea
smokes a pipe
and watches me
sunken into the wedge
of hospital bed

My Skeleton sits
in the visitor's chair
in the corner of room
crunched, continues to wait
listening to the deflated sound
of my breathing

I am nothing—
an empty rice bag
missing my bones

My skeleton
with her curved ivory
and metal clamps
that go from neck to hips

She slurps her tea
blows smoke rings at me
a smoke that dragons
a dragon she mouth-puppets
when she deigns to speak
her voice hoarse
horses without tongues

My skeleton blinks
with no eyes
as I eat bland rice
trying to fill the empty
space
she smiles
with all her pearly
shadow-teeth

My skeleton
sags
helpless and watches
as I muscle through
another spasm
learn how to walk again
my skeleton watches
and waits, and I wonder
when she will take me
back again

Self-portrait
After an Epidural

Days like these and
I channel my tortoise shell spirit
Skin an ancient leatheriness
my eyes watch through body crevice
mask and bouffant cap
guarding away the winds
I rise before dawn
moving slowly towards the sun
I cling to the shell of my belongings
I sleep deeply below ground
and only ever weep
when it is raining

Pain, Capital P

Sometimes I am dumb with pain
Forgetting how to pronounce my own name
Other times I am nauseous with it, dry heaving
Empty stomach, how I greet the day
Days I am muscle cramped-up past walking
Times when auras spin cloud glitter
In the sides of my eyes
Bright migraine pinching the nerves
From ear to elbow, funny bone tingle
Thuds so I drop things
Have difficulty lifting spoon to eat

I have been sad with pain
Brain-chemically depressed by it
I have cried and winced the wet-hot from my eyes
Shouted at those I love because they promised
To keep listening to my leaking tear ducts

Numb in the hum of me
I can disassociate
Exist as unremembered body
Drowning the whole
Drowned in the sounds of my brain
Screaming Ow-Ow-Ow!
Have more squeaky ouch-wheels
Than grease to give
My palms raw from rubbing
More tired than grit

I smile
As my mouth twitches with it

Pain

My pill to swallow, my breathing
Rhythm, my bellyache
My mouth, pain in my mouth
Every word I spit to speak

Tooth, blood, spittle

IV of Swords

The Way Willful Neglect Burns Through Like California Wildfire

A meager medicine poured over a burning fire. The cup was full
to start, but between every set of hands, water sheds so, all I have
left is drops. Licking the bottom of the bucket, the pail, the barrel.
Then they send me the bill, for the entire fill, my hands now empty
tins collecting, begging alms off those I love. So, I put a pin in my
care, like the dead wings of butterfly specimen, clip the few leaves I
have, the bitter fruit, hard and unripe. As this earth, I too am being
milked for conditions beyond anyone's decision. This is the nature of
American spoonie life, this abyss of pain, this Pandora's box within
that opens up to horror show after horror show, mouth coughing
up wound that won't heal, consuming gauze without end. And all
I want to do is say nice things like other children do, but days go
clattering like dominos—cataclysmic with less control, and I fall out
of time, don't know which direction to run in this wilderness, until
all sense is gone, until the forest has fallen, every tree, without any
aplomb. Both person and place gone, everything demolished, there
is no story, nothing to say.

Overlapping Venn Diagrams

My dad and I are stuck in midweek rush hour traffic—
the AC doing nothing for the tension of another bad
appointment, another recommendation for surgery
and there we are in the carpool lane, immovable wall
of cars, when I notice the vehicle in front of us, a black
Maserati with license plate that reads: CT SRGRN
meaning that at least someone is happy, benefiting from
mine and others' bad news, bills that flood in like a fury
and I think did they perform the surgery themselves?
To remove their own heart? And where do they keep it,
and is it in a container as glossy and expensive as this one?

Nothing but the Bells

Low in the belly, a lolloping half gallop
tongue drip wagging, oh how the dogs love
the sound of bells, the tintinnabulation
that means dinner is served!

The dogs had other vague memories
of a mother, of her warm and soft body
of a tumult of puppy brothers and sisters
and the family they lived with, happy children
laughing, the chase of a red striped ball!

And when they arrived here, they had vague
memories of that as well, of how they had tried
to love Pavlov. To nuzzle him with their wet noses
to yip and whine for his attention, to wag their tails
but now, now they knew: nothing but the bells
their new mother, their only love!

The River of Styx and Stones

After the last round of floods
I gave up eating meat again
when millions of animals died
with no escape plan.

Their blood turning rivers red
with the sludge of their bodies.

I stopped eating meat after
I read the article about how
it was the same at prisons,
no escape plan—*how?*

It was two women with disabilities
chained up, in the back of an abandoned
cop car, that died from the cold,
the cold blood in people's hearts.

Hand-Me-Downs

Hand-me-downs feel different
within the disabled community
people don't outgrow their crutches—
their wheelchairs, their oxygen tanks—
they just don't need them anymore
and this is either very good, or
very bad news.

The walker I use belonged to a man
beloved by his wife—widow who
gave it to me, when my legs went out,
after they lost to cancer. Daily I think
how lucky, how unlucky I am
to have it.

How I Hide

Hide in the closet of our dorm room
in the forest between classes
hide my weed in a tobacco pouch
spliffs I smoke to function
within the rigid angles I've been dealt

How I hide down the alley
from the bars on nights I hardly drink
but am often stalked into the shadows by people
wanting to bum off my good time

How I hide the medicine
on airplanes and buses, long car rides
How I hide in pockets of time
count the time in puffs, spritz
to smell of anything else
anyone else

How I hide in hotel bathrooms
towel stuffed under the door
trying to navigate the no-smoking policies
lighting incense as I sit on the toilet seat
or on the floor, smudging pine oil
as a misplaced blessing

How I hide in the backyard, or in
the garage between dinner and dessert
at family gatherings, the birthday candles wait
as I convince my body of its own hunger
as the whipped cream on pumpkin pie
deflates

How I hide
between doctor's appointments
and surgeries, how I hide it in the chocolate
or little drops, or in the tea, or tea bags
or in the bottom of a coffee can
under my tongue
a joint in my bra, a joint in my sock,
a joint in my shoe
and back-pockets
even in the words I do
and don't speak

I hide in my own mouth
and nobody is the wiser

Yolk: Albumen: Shell

Parts of me are old
(bone graft and metal)

Parts of me still young
(newly-formed scars
an influx of hormones)

Parts of me gone numb
(fingertips on this
keyboard)

The light that shines through

onto the yellow wallpaper of my
dreamed up house, is peeling.
The wooden floorboards look nice
but they squeak at every misstep.
There is a skunk in the garden
that digs up any new flowers I
plant; ranunculus, the narcissus
bulbs, round ovals in my hands
makes a real stink if I try to chase
him away by switching the lights
on and off, banging pans, but
I am the one left alone, scared.
The attic has a noise in it that
rattles a fine coat of plaster dust
I find after the Santa Ana winds
roll through. I keep scrubbing at
the walls, scratching at the dirt
with index finger, splinters,
sniff for mold, the yellow flakes
in my hand. Rubbing my hands
together, they won't clean, dots
little yellow confettied pulp
that cakes my skin, sticks to
me, covers me like papier-mâché
little specks of left-over glue
adhering to my nervous and
sweated saltiness, until I am left
perfect—a paper doll, a new piñata
waiting to spill open handfuls
of chewing gum and candies.

Making Space: Small Pieces I Feed the Earth

Surgery is the wound that can save you—
an inversed sculpture, a practice of erasure
a fierce editing of what is,
negotiating what isn't.

But there is only so much the knife can do
so, I dig my heels in rich soil,
sit in the sun as though I am a flower blooming.

The High Priestess

Experimental Fairytale

Dream first of water,
body rounded at the edge,
smear of blurred sensation

Let your body float there,
spin a web of memory
on spider-silk thread

Remember your favorite children's
storybook, then say the word *drought*—
now think of an ocean's ghost

Can you recall Poseidon
once a god, now myth

Picture the mermaid
who has grown frog legs,
though she has nowhere
to swim

Please know your handsome
prince may have his own fish to fry,
dragons to slay and
that the hourglass is indeed full
of quicksand

Fact: in the ashes of their own disaster
dinosaurs grew wings

A phoenix feeds a fire just as
the phoenix needs this fire

We all have to operate within
a certain internal paradox—
it's just that we've lost the manual

Now begin again: translate
from French to Latin
as you fill out one final, brief
survey to earn your daily bread,
your cup of sugar

Clutched in My Fist the Bag I Carry
after Tim O'Brien's short story, "The Things They Carried."

Carries keys to car, front door, small room with bed
stash of meds to swallow, Chapstick that wets the lips,
sunglasses that cut the California glare, matches—

Or a light, the wallet that says: who, what, when, where
and how much, a phone: fishing line tied to photos and friends
voicemail, text, ink pen, square of paper, a borrowed book—

Packet of tissue, which serves as emergency sanitary napkin,
stuffing for the unfulfilled bra, stuffing open-ended wounds
soaking up the tears, plugging up bloodied bent noses—

Blotting watercolor sunsets, un-smudging blurred lines
leaving him dear John note, or to get the next number, recipe
favorite quote, muffling ears because the yelling won't stop—

Anxious folding origami animals, sopping up the spilled everything
flammable enough to stuff the Molotov cocktail, or dampen with
water to cover mouth, the only way forward is through the fire—

The Magician's Assistant

Sews herself back up every night, backstage, after
the show, after the spell's worn off, the makeup and
glitter, the stage lights dimmed, she sits at her mirror
bent over her own figure, needle pulling thread.

The operation as routine as square knots, she will
stand, rub blood out of wound, take a plug of whisky,
and a pull off something often unmentioned.
Smoke spiraling as she readies herself

to sharpen the saw, to clean and oil the toothed
edge—glistening. She prepares for tomorrow's show
where a new room full of strangers will gather—
gasp, open mouthed.

In suspense, half believing, half not, as the magician
cleaves her in two, the applause is for his miracle
and not hers—though it is her body they watch, her body
they imagine long after the popcorn has gone stale.

There is no Time to Learn French

There is no time to fold paper birds.

For 250 days I wear the machine, grateful,
my own heart too weak to do this work alone—
this business of healing. My bones blending
where before there was no-bone, now an alchemy
as the dead breathe life back into my body,
shocked to be holding any shape besides collapse.

There is no time to accessorize.

I strap the bone densifying machine
around my waist, the same routine at the same time
everyday. Careful to line the magnetic waves
with my wound, trying to fuse, trying to become one
being—for good measure, I synch the Velcro tight,
pushing the ON button with its little *beep-beep!*
and I let myself believe *this is working*.

There is no time to be patient.

Because I know life. Life is more precious
than high prices paid, days spent in PT stretching
every last nerve, building new muscle along the spine,
posing for x-rays, reciting Velvet Underground lyrics to myself
as the MRI machine loudly *clacks*, counting backwards
from ten into oblivion—bleed, puke, cold sweat
shed tears, shout, become shattered fragments
of the self—everything once imagined, planned, dreamed of.
Having to inventory all my inner pixels of existence
mosaic a new possibility.

There is no time to fall in love.

Though when I see you carrying all our gear from the car
to our spot in the campground, I wonder if it is okay to slow down.
When you build up the fire, while I settle down to put on the
Spine-ologic machine the insurance company stalled in granting me,
I notice the robin building her nest, darting from twig
to branch to dried grasses back to the branch above our heads,
planning for a future out of the minutia: scrap of moss
loose piece of thread, and the *bee-ep, bee-ep!* reminding me
I need to change out the batteries.

No there is no time to learn French.

Instead, I readily describe my bowel movements
to the inquiring nurses diligently scribbling their notes,
checking to see if the drainage tube is still leaking wound,
bags measured and emptied every six hours, twenty ounces
of blood flushed down the toilet. What remains is my body,
a body that takes the stitches, that fresh-skin scars over, finds
a way to begin anew. Painstakingly drains the thousand tiny
needle pricks left of my skin, of any doubt. And I become someone
who survives, with words and more words, promises to survive,
whittled down to necessity, like the best lines in any love note.

Music

Playing every note at once
isn't music

It is the same with cooking
and all the ingredients at
your disposal

As with love
and all the blood
in your heart

Remember, when you can
this is your time
on a planet every generation
must reuse

A hand-me-down
a gift
where we all belong

Peaches Three Ways

One
Buy an extra peach, at least one
may turn between now and when
you have time to make the pie.

And please, no need to doubt the sun's
ferociousness, it is hotter than fire,
hotter than laser beams, illuminates
our solar system without expectation.

Two
When you feel like an immovable
rock, let everything else be water
pushing away all your untidy edges
the stone-pit at the center of the fruit.

Today is neither good nor bad
like a peach grown, or grown moldy
it just is, and like this, you are also.

Three
The day after my sister died, I found
myself in the Merrill College Garden
under the orchard's canopy as I fed my
aunt and mother peaches, thinking *Huh.*

Because I knew then, as I know now:
*this is the best peach I have, and ever
could have tasted:* sun-warm, fresh,
seconds from the branch, my mother's
face, my aunt's.

Love Doesn't Always Glimmer Like a Horse

love doesn't always marry
sometimes it dies young
leaves children behind
love doesn't always last
gets traded away before
we know what we had
love passes in the look
in the feel of hands intertwined
love blisters and warts
sags with the weight of
all that is not love
love is insecure, ties
its shoes with double knots
wears a helmet and elbow pads
love is the one stuck with arrows
asking you kindly to apply
pressure to the wounds

Your Mouth Is a Cutting Board—Mine Is a Knife

My sister is a teacup with
shark teeth brewing, my niece
is a squid, a helicopter, a castle
a pink bear puppet on her hand.

My best friend is a pelican,
my best friend is a watermelon,
my best friend slices the bread.

I can't read braille
but it feels right
to the touch.

The way your mouth
opens and closes
your eyes blink, your
nose scrunches.

My father is a suitcase
full of technicolor photographs.

My brother once ate my birthday cake
and that really made me cry.

I can tell my rabbit
doesn't like me, but likes
when I let him loose
in the grass, scratches a bit
when it's time to put him
back in his hutch.

The fish tank is full of piranha
well—two of them, and as they eat
the other fish, I stare at their
wide-jutted, thorn-toothed grins.

Grasshopper on the branch
startle the pants out of me
and when I see the worm
in the soil, fat vein, I'm always
sure that I've struck oil.

You'll know when I've been an ocean
if there is still sand on my tongue.
Pull me from the waters—a broken wave
pockets full of crab claws, clam
shell, kelp in my hair.

Remember you can drown a rose
in fresh water—but I am not a rose.

New Love

My scar; long divide down the spine,
explicit trauma on display,
bathing suit exposing, or tank top revealing
where sutures have been.

My scar, now multiple surgeries deep,
marks the path I walk, the miles
to go before I sleep, the hours
I've had to cry, sweat, bleed, beg
this life for another chance.

This scar: the only way I know how to love
all those who trust me, have given me
blood, cadaver bone, seat, tears.

Let this scar show all there is to tell,
an openly worn story, my brutality clear,
my beauty: not the face that launched
a thousand ships, but the heart that takes
a thousand arrows.

X of Wands

Of Poems & Folded Promises

Medical bills stacked in batches, surgery
questionnaires surveying—making me data—
medical appointment cards and calendar listings,
insurance denials and explanation of benefits,
begin to pillar

Like an eccentric's haphazard
stack of reread books, toppling over in slow
motion, scattering papers everywhere,
a snow globe of dissatisfaction nearly
smothering me, choking, and I want to
give in, let myself be buried in these loose
sheets, become—myself—confetti.

When blank scrap of envelope, drops
in hand with a pen I write, is it these words?
Were there others? Insist this all happened
to someone, there is a wild heart beating wildly
and wildly I add this to my shrine, collecting
poems & folded promises—hopes for better
times.

Wearing an Armband with my Name, Date of Birth, and Scannable Barcode

I pace the length of the hospital's pre-surgery gallery.
It is not nerves so much as not wanting to tense up.
After all, I know just how much muscle they will have
to cut to get at the bone, and like with any other meat,
I'm told the tenderer slice goes down all the sweeter.

So, I walk back-and-forth, past the row of predawn windows
and again, past the black-and-white portraits of Hollywood stars
in the reflected light of so much fragile glass I take my own picture.
I let myself be grateful for the miracle of breathing,
and for all the amazing mechanics within.

We're Not Quite Friends

But I know the nurse's name. The name of her cat. That she got in
a fight with her husband last night, an argument she'll return to
at the end of her day. Her daughter is in college now, and last year
she let her hair go grey. She tells me she likes my teal DIY dye-job.
Asks me what new book I am reading. Helps me with my pregnancy
test.

The Physician's Assistant has grown a big red beard that hides
behind his Covid mask. I think he thinks it makes him look older. It
doesn't. He and his wife, a pediatrician, have set up a hummingbird
feeder to ease the loneliness of quarantine. The birds like to eat
lunch as the couple eats their lunch. When I tell him about my pain,
that I don't want narcotics, and am not ready for the next surgery
he believes me. He listens.

The receptionist at my Physical Therapist's shares cat videos with
me on her phone that make us laugh. She tells me how she is happy
for her sister who is getting married, but she will miss sharing a
home, clothes, and makeup. Her lunches always smell the best when
she reheats them in the microwave to eat at the table near the big
front windows bathing her in natural light. We compare notes on
caring for 3 rescue cats as I sip the coffee she has prepared in the
waiting area.

The Pharmacist Assistant with her abundance of well-coordinated
jewelry twinkles and chimes from behind the counter as she
sanitizes it for each person. She keeps an order of assembled pens,
pencils, and sharpies, at the ready, clipped in the seam of her button-
up collared blue shirt. She knows all the meds I take, how often, and
at what dosage. She notices days I use my cane or use my walker.
Always asks how I am doing.

The checkout woman at the corner store went to visit her only grandchild last week. Her daughter lives now in Seattle. The boy just turned four. With work and expenses, she doesn't know when she'll get to visit again but her daughter plans to come down soon. When she changes her lipstick, it is to a brighter red though now it has been two years since I've seen her mouth; she smiles at me with her dark brown eyes. She knows when my cats are hungry. My time of the month. That I don't dig on sweets and have switched my regular drink from white wine to whisky and sparkling mineral water on ice.

We're none of us quite friends. When I can though, I bring them fresh ripe plums from the farmers market or a spare joke, if I have it.

My Feet Thwackadoodle

when I get the epidural
in my low-low back.

My *rushing rivers*,
the acupressure points below
the big toes, get inundated
with all the lost *messages*
from these past weeks.

The numbness now flickers up and down my legs
restless as butterflies kicking broken glass in the night
telegraph notes sent along the nervous system,
burn like bonfire, wishes whispered into the night
across ocean.

After weeks of missed signals
I only hear from this *smoke*
can only scrape up these *ashes*
that go *thwak, thwak, thwak.*

If I had a god to beg to, it would be
to ameliorate this soil, to believe
even *this is possible.*

They tell me there is a *science* now
to feed my own blood back to my body,
the platelets nourishing deep within,
my *ocean* floor could be replenished.

I ask my doctors,
who recommend this medicine,
to keep begging the insurance companies
who we all know, try everything to deny
and delay all of my *claims.*

My mother asks me when I will have
my next injection, she is the one who leaves
circles in the park, restless, waiting to hear

when can she take her one remaining daughter
home.

She isn't complaining, she is just asking
if I'll keep doing *everything* I can to survive.

Left Thigh

I'm trying to convince my Left Thigh to flex, to push past
the numbness and infuse feeling into the flesh,
but Left Thigh is having none of it. The prolonged
concentration beading sweat on my brow, and still the action
is only murmurs of *fizzles out.*

Yes, Left Thigh hardly yawns or blinks, ignores both heat and ice
and the deep cat scratches accumulate—my own hands become a stranger,
hot tears and anger stream down my face as I grasp at straws.

Imagine Left Thigh, you are not—not made of tissue, tendons, and sinew.
Let the marrow in your bone melt, imagine you are composed instead
of fistfuls of flowers blooming today's begonias.

And like a dreaming dog, Left Thigh twitches—
like a child suddenly paying attention.

And so, I raise my voice up again. Everyday a new story. This one goes:
you are made of gingko leaves yellow fanning, a rustle in November's
wind, and Left Thigh flies a kite.

I say Left Thigh you are not, have no legs at all, rather
a mermaid's glossy tail, rhinestone bright beneath the water,
and Left Thigh swims.

Soon, Left Thigh exhibits magical powers, says to me today is not
a cold day, wind pricking up goosepimpled skin. No, Left Thigh is warm,
feels a wind cloudy with pollen, late in the spring. The twist of birds,
Kingfisher snatching at the air. Left Thigh wears these costumes
like a skin beneath the skin.

Now Left Thigh can go out dancing, the night made of sequins and velvet,
just the right amount of glitz. Left Thigh twirls and steps, never tires
though the rest of me slinks back, exhausted.

The memory of what Left Thigh was before may blip—
faint cry of homing beacon lighthousing through space,
but under the pool of numbness, Left Thigh becomes all of their desires:
flower, yellow fanning, twist of birds, a true shapeshifting sophisticate.

To Describe this Body I Invent

When pain scoops eyes out of my intention,
I call this a *Swiss cheese headache*
and my worsening clumsiness
are *the dropsies*, mornings where my coffee
spills all over, dishes break as I try to clean.
Walking while leaning against a wall
or walking the perimeter of the room so there is
always something to grab hold of is *furniture walking*.

The way my neck feels blocked up
as the air pressure changes before a storm—
these are *predictions of rain*
and *thwakadoodling* is the way my feet
go from numb to sensations of broken glass and hot pokers.
Sour-guts: the way my belly aches after days of
heightened symptoms, feels like I'm about to puke—
farts are *tootie birds* ready to escape my butt.

Spasms are spasms
but some are Charlie horse bad, stuck
like my body is pulling itself apart string by string,
and can make it easy to pass out.
My blood pressure drops as I lose vision,
must lie myself down quickly before gravity overtakes
my weak and curved bones, this is *what scares me.*

The latest diagnosis is called *perimenopause*—
is the reason I am having night sweats and month-long
periods, the blood thicker than before
the weight gain, the hot flashes.
My body is burning and then again made from these ashes.

Poem Without a Name

Some days, love, I am built like a guillotine—
nothing you say can save you. My mouth,
gravity's weapon, blade's sharp chop. My glance,
blank ouroboros stare. My eyes glassy—
a one-way mirror staring contest, determined
to end this, because my head rolls.

The more I want our future together,
the more I have to accept this truth—
that my bad days are becoming yours.
Days where it's hard to move, slow to walk,
tight in my bones, achy tug-numb stuck—
days where even your vise-grip foot rubs
won't make a dent in my rock-spasms.

Days between diagnosis, pictured in black
and white digitized scans, photocopied
anxious bristled nerves. How to explain,
how to pour the doctor's words into your ears
without causing a flood? Without
drowning you, and all those that I love?

So, I stick out my elbows, point my teeth,
thinking it might somehow be easier to twist
this love up into some other shape—call you
friend instead, cut you loose. I think about
how you could see other people, be happy.

I would have time to read and write more,
distract myself, sharpening my blade. Avoiding
the issue, my own problems left unexplained
become less real, disappearing away from
everything. Reassured in my belief that nobody
could love a guillotine.

But you see, it's the bad news I don't want
to share, and you don't waiver, or shake
or blink. Somehow you traverse all my pointed
and shiny broken mirror-like edges, and you hold,
you hold out, and hold on, and you hold onto me.
Sometimes neither of us says the right thing
but we make it up, we make up, we keep on
trying—we keep our mouths open.

Gravity

It takes four screws to the throat
to tell you, to keep telling you
I love you.

This is how I mouth the words
with metal stitched to my bone.
This is how I hold you, big spoon
in the night—

the vice grip that holds the moon
in place, call it gravitational pull.
Call it love.

Letter to My Forgetful Self

run if you must
walk gentle if you can
this earth is the softest
landing place one can
ever hope for

notice who frightens the birds
and who calls them forth
remember dogs only bark
when they can't be soothed

remember the puppies' soft
belly, how they urinate
over everything, how
you once did the same

and if you are very lucky
and don't blow your good hand
you might just get to again

Vulture,

I'm sorry about what has happened to your name. How you have come to mean the reaper when you are just coroner. You, first witness to what has been lost, you formed yourself in the shape of deaths remains so you could carry each body, bone by bone, into the sky. There are tribes of people that prefer this way, ask you to take them also from their place atop hard mountains. I see your black feathers beautiful. Your shape in the sky, a foreshadow, a template in mourning. This is the way you love the dead. This is how you clear the world of carcass and loss, so earth won't choke on blood. You wear a blood mask. Forever grateful to have found your place, your sacred purpose. You are not death, but death's friend. Please, find me when it's time.

Yours,
Meat and Bones.

Knight of Swords

KNIGHT of SWORDS

Rate Your Pain

On a scale of one-to-ten, what does the pain rate today?

You can't claim a *ten*. Remember that is the day marked by
your sister dying before her time, the crumpled shape
of your deflated parents, you and all your surviving siblings
in crisis.

The question is always the same, though when you're asked
at the children's hospital a doll is handed to you. The doll
is teardrop shaped and has a big button attached to it, inscribed
with all the different faces that express each level of pain.

This is the day you grow two inches on the operating table;
the doctors don't know it yet, you're also having an allergic reaction
to the yard-stick's worth of metal they've attached to vertebrae
where the bone chips shaved from right hip have been placed.
You squeeze the doll to your chest that is breathing with a partially
collapsed lung; this is your first *nine*.

This is the day that kicks numbers *one*-through-*four* off the chart,
though you still feel the IV needle sliding in and out of your wrist,
the adhesive tape pulling at fresh stitches—it's become normal to you
that you have the biggest scar many people have ever seen,
even though you yourself have never been able to look directly
at your own wound.

You must instead feel with bare hands in the night, discover
just like anyone, your own body. How that scar changes in ripples
every time the doctors go back in, under the skin. The question is always
the same, though now there is also an outline of a body to fill, shade in the places
that burn, that ache, that go numb, that throb, that spasm. And a list to check:
is it hot pain, or cold pain, intermittent or constant?

You notice there is no box to tick to explain the hit of truth
that there is no getting up and down from the ground now
without assistance, or stepping up the pain a bump, and
chairs are worse, feel like deathtraps designed to torment,
always too long, or too short, or digging into that space between
metal and fusion.

What number the grief in having to let go
of everything that weighs more than newborn niece,
including any plans to ever have your own child?

There are lucky days, days you use the five fingers of hands to grip cane
or walker, to keep from falling, or jiggering the arthritis that's developed.
To move even if it's slow like the old, the way time sticks in its heels
when counting down the months till you must schedule surgery again
slow enough—you find new pleasures—watching the slow-petal-open
blossom of rooted succulent. This you don't rate but enjoy, simple
like when your love brews you coffee while you a take shower,
the way your cats purr and cuddle no matter the hour.

The tests the doctor ordered this week even she admits
will be painful. Asks if you've ever been shocked by a bug zapper.
Knowing already how hard it is to walk it back from the all-encompassing
bewilderment of a *nine*, to walk at all—you end up grateful
for all those moments just between the *sixes, sevens, eights.*

In My Nearly Nine Years Applying
for Disability Recognition

The notices come at random. Just another slip of paper
determining my fate, or what my fate is worth.
To all the lever pullers out there, all those gear grinders,
chewing their bitter lives, pointing their long fingers at me.
Trying to pull through it all on less than $10,000 a year
in LA where all my doctors live. Their offices all top-floor offices,
where I wait with my thumbs twirling, taking in the views
with the tears at the back of my eyes ready to spill
at the news.

What pain, another day, and yet my bones are kinder
than those that continue to deny me my meager portion.
Just a sliver or slice, I ask, and only from the richest pie on the planet.
Grubby hands that are made to beg on top of caring for myself—
more wound than body. After looking at all my naked diagnosis,
every slice and stitch, all they do is send me another survey
to ask, *but how do you really feel?*

The Old Man's Boss Isn't the Boss's Old Man

The old man's boss has kept him late, away
from kid's ball game and recital, has been paid
to pay him less, clocked and calculated the hours,
the meatloaf left cold on the counter, the house
dark as he eats alone.

The boss's old man has cancer. Has been in hospital
over the holiday. The boss curls up with him in
the hospital bed even though it is against regulation
and the boss knows all about regulations, as it stands,
they are both missing his mother who would know
what to do now. And next.

The old man's boss tried to explain automation
is inevitable, that hours would have to be cut,
but the old man knows robots won't pay taxes,
that things will be grim from now on and he stays
late again because he's not sure what else he can do.
He is calculating the next three months of bills,
estimating the interest rate and limit on his next
credit card.

The boss's old man hates cheese. But hates being
picky even more. Something about the way he was
raised, teaching him to suffer more than he needed.
To stuff his feelings in his shirt pockets because how
dare he. It's what gave him his edge. It's what he
taught his son, though he wouldn't admit it, wouldn't
know how. The boss takes care to stop by every
morning with the old man's favorite bear claw, before
he opens shop where he shuts down, shuts up.

The old man's boss just called him in again. He'll
have to sing happy birthday via video conference, they
have that technology now, can blow out the candles
remotely. When the screws get tighter, he does not call
himself a robot but he has been dreaming in binary,
speaking in code.

The boss's old man has gone fishing but isn't catching much.

The old man's boss keeps tugging on his necktie.

The boss's old man throws his Jell-O at the nurse.

The old man's boss hasn't been sleeping well, neither has
the old man.

The boss's old man fills out his advanced directive.

The old man's boss forgets to tuck in his shirt
but tells the old man he needs to get a haircut.

The boss's old man wishes things were different.

The old man's boss just wants the same.

And the old man doesn't know what he's gonna do
if things don't change.

We Smile
after WS Merwin's "Thanks"

We smile
behind our masks, we smile
the corners of our eyes crinkle
in passing maybe we wave
maybe we don't
but from six feet away we smile

300 thousand dead here
in their coffins, smiling six feet underground
the funeral hall is empty
the hearse rides alone, yet we smile
through computer screens facing
in all directions our smiles
replicated across the internet
glowing in someone else's living room
we smile

The forest is burning again
the trees birthday candles lit
what wish could blow it out
what a year it has been
we have not hugged our brothers
in months and months and yet
we smile and scoop up the cat
nuzzle and nuzzle in our frazzled state
the sanitized space alienating us from
our next-door neighbor
who is yelling at 9 in the morning
at their spouse, again, puppy
cowering in the corner
and we smile

someone once told us
that we need no guarantee
no contract with the sun
that it will rise and set
our moon just as steady
these days we are not sure
that we believe them
but we smile
and we smile
hoping against hope

Cause and Effect

What is this invisible force that hits
so powerful in my life it bends my spine,
leaves me doubled over into a permanent
squiggle—hard as any bus or bullet?
My misfortune is not knowing what
to change or not to change. Scoliosis is

an idiopathic disorder most prevalent
in adolescent girls, teenagers captive to
our anatomies, teens so often belittled
growing up in a culture steeped in
misogyny, assault, and rape. Maybe we
are just trying to make ourselves smaller,
uglier in a way, hoping nobody will notice
we are here. Maybe we just needed
at one point, to be held up, like we really
really mattered.

Or maybe it's our own internal gravity
weighing us down, asking us to fly
to the moon, all the way to Mars, asking us
to escape.

modern robot

scoliosis recomposes
vertebrae: the wavering
arrow, now a trident
the spine aligned to a tuning fork
finding water, fish bones from hips

the moon demands
the tide pulls in
dreams the color of rust
unfolding the winding coastline
run here until it fractures
the nightmares of
car crash, whip-lash
fear of the breaks

the torso cast
corset with teeth
has metal clasps
pulled tight, strain
tears the bed sheets

survival is trade with the sandman
trade in stainless steel rods
for titanium double-helix
in case of polar shift
the North star has been slipping
fear of lightning into the punch
take a long drink, this looks like
dancing in the rain, IV drops
a smoothness into the vein

headphones cure the headaches
sift through the waves
like a modern robot
holding the clock
radio so the signal gets
clearer, the antennas implanted
in the body double as titanium pillars
pillars sifted from sand, fishhooks
feel like salt, electric wire

give up touching metal
to avoid the static shock
from being metal
an ungrounded instrument
internal battery sparks
shudders the whole body

swell up
against old scars
moving every cell
like an ocean
an always
contortionist

balance, visualize
a bowl of fire, inside
the body remembers
how to feel, learns to
lay down on the wooden
floor, the piano is
being played, echoes
through the deck
of this vessel

made of water
made of rust

The Prize

I had to explain to the surgeon
that I wanted to keep the metal
after it had been removed

It's not that I wanted it
just knew that somehow
I had earned it, and couldn't bare
to have it buried as biohazard waste
or in the ground before
and without me

These metal
bolts and washers
two thin rods
odd-machined sculpture
bent to the curves
in the lean and slouch
of my posture
scaffolding to keep me
up-right, assembled
into and now out of
my muscled ribs

This collection of titanium bling
I will keep it with the other set
the stainless steel from the first surgery
that metal that I am allergic to, that
boiled and blistered
I have saved these   things
keep them in   odd drawer

There are other relics
the neck braces, the x-rays
the wrist bands, cotton balls
Steri-Strips

It is the metal though that I must
clean methodically, soak in bleach
scrub with old toothbrush and rag
in my latex gloves, hold each piece
to the sun, see how it shines
in the light

I examine them
read the little
letters and numbers
imprinted in each
I will keep them
and maybe one day
melt them down

into a chalice	for ceremony
into a vase	for flowers
into an urn	for ashes
into a teapot	for company

a paper weight	charm
a music box	lullaby
a pair of scissors	craft
a trophy	wins
counterfeit coins	trade
a crown	glorifies
Eureka!	

If like metals spill the same amount of water
from a filled container, the body must transcend
its own internal displacement in order to maintain
a sense of wholeness, the hard immovable part
of the self that will in all ways need every spare caress

The metal that appears the contents
of junk-drawer, through process of osmosis
has absorbed an intrinsic quality, has become
something precious, to me the metal, now
externalized, clutched to my chest, creates
a kind of pressure, reversing its alchemy
until I am only grasping straw

Queen of Swords

QUEEN of SWORDS

If a Poem Was a Dress

Sometimes when I can't find a happy way to see myself
like when I'm having a hard time getting out of bed
or figuring out how to get dressed for another day of it,
I have to let go of me all together. I pretend it isn't me
but a poem, a poem scrubbing its face in the morning mirror
a poem pulling up its socks, shocking the world in mismatched
fuchsia pink polka-dots and chartreuse zig-zag striped toes,
a poem distracted as the cats curl, one by my feet, one up on
my lap, warm bundles of purrs, forgetting my makeup
forgetting to pin back my hair, forgetting to be.

Sitting in the Coffeeshop

I've ordered and as I wait for
my cappuccino I unpack my rolling papers,
my gram of White Widow freshly
purchased at the counter. The skunky
smell of the flowers, sticky in my fingers
as I press them into the shape, hand roll
a joint. My drink served, I sit and sip,
draw in my travel journal, light up
inhale, listen to the DJ, who doesn't even
lift an eyebrow at me. Here, out in the open
nobody shouts hate, nobody dies
and the pain quiets, and I'm okay
for a little while, I'm okay.

Quartet

Corkscrew sunsets
Insistent cat cuddle
Head butts
Knocking pen askew
*

My mother borrowing
The knife sharpened with
Admiration for the ease
Of a sharp blade
*

The sounds of dinner
Tapping against the kitchen counter
Cutting board, sharp smell of green
Onions and earthy mushrooms
*

I dream of paralysis
I dream of running through parks
I dream of large birds

The KB-Z Operating Manual

Everyday tell me two truths and a lie,
blink twice if you mean it, tap your nose if you don't.

Make the coffee strong and black, exchanging
revolutionary facts between sheets, between shifts.

Write a list of favorite words to recite as pillow talk, practice
acupressure points on my tired toes, worn nerves.

Love collecting rocks, finding pressed flowers in the pages
of your books, chosen feathers, the wizzah of dawn.

Nap all day or notice how the light shifts through the window
curled up on the sofa as you read a novel all the way through.

Talk poems with me and listen to Hepcat, Desmond
Dekker, Toots, Junior Murvin, Tenor Saw.

Make up secret handshakes, write your own vows, promise
you'll only spend time on the stories you want to tell.

My Name

1. My name, Kelsey,
meaning the wind off an island,
sometimes an ocean breeze, shade
under lank palm to cool the sun
sandy day.

Sometimes ferocious, cold chop
storm whipping fast into a hurricane
a name being choked out
as each island—

rare bird feather, tropical fruit grove,
volcanic stone, desert, hundred-year-old
tortoise shell, buried treasure—sinks
into the waters of a rising ocean.

My name, now a warning call, *Kelsey!*
extinguished as all this earth drowns.

2. I wonder what the name is
for the wind that's generated by
the combustion of bombs, or the name
for wind over a newly-dug grave.

I wonder what the name is
for the wind that kicks up a dust,
and the wind that comes drifting
heavy with mist. I wonder if
there is a name for the wind that first
compels a given bird to fly. Or
the name for the wind that is heavy
with the sound of bees, migrating.

The name for spring's first wind
and fall's. The name for the wind
with the first snow, the first rainbow
of the year.

I wonder what the name is. If
there is a name. Like *Bullwazzle*.
That's the name of the wind
that blows on April Fool's Day.
Fool!

Cornswaple, that's the name
for the harvest wind. And *Moonswine*,
that's the name for the wind
with a superstitious streak. And
Burdleberry. That's the name
of the wind that's for best picking
wildflowers in. And, during the first rain
of the year, *Thenakedrun* is the name
for the wind drummed up by the thumping
wet bodies of hundreds of UC Santa Cruz
students running, around campus in only
their sneakers.

Coddletint, always comes before
lightning. And *Crapdangit, Crapdangit!*
the wind that makes technology
go haywire. A *Hoozananny*
is the best wind for swapping
a bottle of wine around in.
Punperpancake, the wind that smells
of waffles and beckons brunch.

I want to know the names,
all the names, and fly a kite in them,
every day I can.

On the Other Side of the Blade

I cut and I cut
The *thud-knife* sound
Against the bamboo cutting board

I cut the vegetables
And I pretend that they are me

Cut-thud the heads off broccoli
Cut-thud the onions into little bits
Of perfect Russian doll parts
And press the garlic like tears

I cut and I feel myself
On the other side of the blade
The edge curves like my spine
Cut-thud, into the deep end of muscle
Cut-thud to bone
Lumbar
Thoracic
Cervical
Ribs
Pelvis
Sacral
Bone soup

I cut the limes
Into fourths
Push-squeeze my thumbs
Into the juicy rinds
Like eyes
Parched & angry

Pressed Flowers

marigolds spring forth
the past overlapped with a layer of time
like earth and how we dig it

sweet peas are family
how a favorite person lost
no longer knits me slippers
uncut apples circles without star shapes in them

the sunflowers Robert planted
in places I never thought could grow
while my flax seeds have only just sprouted
taking so long to grow out of season

did I tell you?
we picked wildflowers on your birthday
I mean dug up trailside sprouts and brought them home
to watch them bloom, which some did

blossomed like the geraniums in my favorite singer's hair
bougainvillea in my favorite artist's braids
a daisy behind a favorite lover's ear, the smile
and talk of the life we'll have

in a small vase, a handful of flowers plucked
the week after
father is in the hospital
for the first time

thankfully an easy fix we breathe easier
for now, remember the rosemary,
the garlic, the lemon, the laugh

Body Love

My body loves its soft silences,
equally its loud exhales. My body loves
moaning against my chosen partner
as it rains, as it sun shines, as it hazes over.
My body loves its escapes
like the involved concentration
in growing new flowers
the lost way I feel for soil,
the crumpling of dried leaves,
and unwanted snails.

The discernment this body allows—
to choose this, to pluck a plant to its death,
to allow the grasses and clover to grow,
to burn and water.

I was born under one sign
yet can play with that besides fire.

I water the sunflowers my partner planted.
How tall they are now.
I dig at the old weeds planted two generations ago
without thought for the future,
gather stones and crystals to bring to our home.
I blow out the candles year after year,
proving to faraway planters
the care it takes to still be here.

To care temporarily for my little blip in time—
so I can pass this space on to the next,
so I can say this spot is cared for,
so I can condense into my own grain of stardust,
passing through hourglass.

Do not miss my long hair—
miss me.

This Body

This body will not be burned,
too much metal in me, when I die
put me back into the mountain,
curl my body, simple silk shift
into the earth, nestle me
in the roots of a young tree
so that my spirit may climb
from this place, back to
the sky, cloud float and star dust

For Unknown

I wouldn't recognize
you in a photo
don't know if you
were man or woman
whether you were young
old, or middle-aged

Did you ride a bike
know how to drive
like to fish
drink wine

Did you have children
brothers, sisters
I don't know what
god you prayed to
for who, what, or if you voted

Or what songs
you knew all the words to
the flowers you could name
the place you called home

All I know is
as I speak now
I must insist always
on your kindness
must say something
of what you gave
to this stranger

As part of you
is buried here
in my body
in my neck
where it was breaking
in my back
where it was broken
I fuse to slivers
of your bone
and begin to mend

Were you tall, stout
or medium in height
did you have long hair
or was it kept short
did your hands fix engines
roll out pie crusts
wash dishes, build sandcastles

The doctors
call you cadaver
but I know you are hope
you are chance
an immeasurable gift
more time

I wonder how many
you gave to
are they man or woman
young or old
are they walking
fishing, riding a bike
do they have children
brothers, sisters

Setting the Curve

Yes the outline of breast
the smooth of hip, round thigh, calf flexed

Yes the pregnant belly taught
and the perfect ass walking just so

But also, the spider web of life,
clouds puffering, shape-shifting the skies,
eucalyptus leaf, ginkgo fan

The way your mouth upturns in a smile
when I whisper *I love you*

Pebble and Tide

My heart
Worn sea glass you palm
As you walk the shores

My want
The way wind curls, is
Felt yet, unseen

The sky
My lungs unfurling
As a well-placed sigh

To feel small
Let everything in
Pebble, moon, tide

To feel big
Let the sands loose of
Your grip, grain by grain

My heart
Raw mussel, curved shell
A glimmer in the wrack

Occasionally Pink, or White

As I slow down, everything slows down
as you might expect, words like bird, and flower
and tree, pull themselves apart—unravel.

They become, as I sit by the open window, red
headed house finch, a black phoebe watching for flies,
house sparrows nesting in the roof tiles next-door.

Starlings making such a ruckus, the mocking jays
doing the same, mourning doves pecking at seed
in the grass, goldfinch at the feeder, house wren
in the sage bush, Anna's hummingbird chasing—

Allen's hummingbird chasing after, black-chinned
hummingbird in the hot lips salvia,
as a California sycamore shades us all,
as California poppies bloom iridescent orange
occasionally pink, or white.

If you cut these
and burn the bottoms of their stems, they will
bloom for you daily in a vase, their singed ends
convincing them to go on living, to continue
believing in the power of the sun.

For the Love of What is Holy

For some it will be an insect
A rare butterfly or moth
The way beetles burrow or have strong wings

For others a snail, a mollusk
An octopus, or squid
The mammoth, the whale studying
The extinction of the rhino

For some it will be the smile
On a particular child's face
Or the way a love brushes hair back
From off your brow
The smell of grandmother's cookies

For others it will be the first hand ever
Held open to them with no kickbacks
Expected, or their hard-working moms
Or a favorite pair of shoes ready to take them
Anywhere

For some it may be themselves
Their own breathing
The miracle of having a body
In which to experience life, this planet
Pleasures

For others it will be comic books
And french fries, and greasy stained thighs
Sharing a soda with two straws
Holding hands at the movies
Learning how to drive
Moving their tassels from one side
Of their graduation cap to the other

And still for some it will be respite
A break from all the dishes and mess
And endless to-do lists, a good place to sit
And read a new book, or nap, or watch
Sparrows gather outside spring's
Window

And yet for others it will be nature itself
The tallness of trees, the rush of wind
Being caught in a wave, a swirl of salt water
Cloudy and forever mysterious
Sand between toes
Grass stains and sweat

For me it is you

And for the love of what is holy
All that is holy, I give thanks

THE STAR.

About the Author

This is Kelsey Bryan-Zwick's first full collection of poems, and they are thrilled to be a part of the Moon Tide Press family. Kelsey (she/they) is a queer, bilingual, disabled, American poet based in Los Angeles, California. They are the author of four chapbooks, the most recent being *Bone Water* (Blanket Sea Press) which is a digital and audio collection of fifteen poems on scoliosis. Kelsey writes reviews and interviews for the Los Angeles Poet Society, they also teach poetry workshops and write essays in collaboration with The Poetry Lab. They are Acting Chair of Produced Media for the Stonewall Democratic Club where they advocate for change.

Kelsey is the founder and editor of the micro-press BindYourOwnBooks which creates handmade journals, poetry collections and snail-mail art cards. Kelsey's poetry has been twice nominated for the Pushcart Prize and nominated for The Best of the Net. Their poetry can be read in *Cultural Daily, Cholla Needles, The Rise Up Review, Spillway, Redshift, Right Hand Pointing, Trailer Park Quarterly,* and *Writing in a Woman's Voice.* Kelsey is the Alien Buddha House of Horrors Champion for their short story, "Femme Fatale & The Gun." You can find them on the gram @theexquisitepoet or on the web https://kelseybryanzwick.

Acknowledgements

Thank you to the following publications and editors that have supported and shared my poems, I am humbled by your wisdom and kindness.

"Girl With Scoliosis, Plays Soccer" and "(Mad)woman in the Attic/ Invisible Stones," were first published in *Rise Up Review*.

"Agoraphobia," "Cause and Effect," "Wearing an Armband with my Name, Date of Birth and Scannable Barcode," were first published in *Writing in a Woman's Voice*.

"Kintsugi," was first published by *One Sentence Poems*.

"Scoliosis," and "Just Discovered," were first published in *petrichor*, which also nominated "Scoliosis" for Best of the Net.

"Our Tradition," "Letter to Ansel," "Forgetting the Flowers," "Occasionally Pink, or White," "Making Space: Small Pieces I Feed the Earth," "There is no time to Learn French," "My Feet Thwakadoodle," "To Describe this Body I Invent," "X-Rays, MRIs, CTs, Bone Scans," were published in *Cholla Needles*.

"Senbazuru," and "The Way Willful Neglect Burns Through Like California Wildfire," were published as Moon Tide Press's *Poet of the Month* in May 2020.

"Peaches Three Ways," was first published in *Redshift 2* and "Clutched in my Fist the Bag I Carry," and "Scrambled Eggs," were published in *Redshift 4*.

"Speaking Ill," was published *in Lummox 9*.

"Love Doesn't Always Glimmer Like a Horse," "Sister," "Sitting in the Coffeeshop," and "Hand-Me-Downs" were first published by *Right Hand Pointing*.

"New Love," was first published in *Incandescent Mind: Selfish Issue*.

"Your Mouth is a Cutting Board/ Mine is a Knife," was first published in *Cadence Collective* and was later published in *Trailer Park Quarterly*.

"If a Poem Was a Dress," "Music," and "For the Love of What is Holy," were first published in *Ponder Savant*.

"The Old Man's Boss Isn't the Boss's Old Man," was first Published in *The Alien Buddha Destroyed the Economy*.

"Poem Without a Name," and "The Magician's Assistant," were first published in *Making Up Poems* an anthology by Picture Show Press.

"Sometimes the Knives," was published in *Spillway 2020*.

"Pebble and Tide," was published by The Love of Words in the anthology, *Short Poems Ain't got Nobody to Love*.

"Setting the Curve," "Of Poems & Folded Promises," and "Experimental Fairytale" were first published in *Eunoia Review*.

"Self-portrait" was first published in *Bold Monkey* and *Bone Water*.

"Idiopathic Curvature," "Under the Bone Saw," "Waking Up in Hospital," "Left Thigh," and " Anatomy of Noise," were first published in the chapbook *Bone Water*. "Left Thigh" was also nominated by Blanket Sea Press for the Pushcart Prize.

"Admission," and "For Unknown," were first published in *Cadence Collective*, and *Watermarked*.

"Body of Art," was first published in *Like a Girl: Perspectives on Feminine Identity*.

"The ransom notes," was published in *East Jasmine Review*.

"The light that shines through," The *Camel Saloon's International Women's Day Issue*

"The Prize," was published in the *Camel Saloon* where it was the editor's choice for the month, as well as in *Watermarked*.

"Overlapping Venn Diagrams," "Nothing but the Bells," and "The River of Styx and Stones," were published in *Bold Monkey*.

"Left Thigh," "Scoliosis," and "New Love" were published alongside a review of *Bone Water* in *Cultural Daily*.

In Thanks

I give thanks for the land, to the Tongva region from which I write. It is the planet that makes all possible and as mama earth gives us her body for existence, it is for her body I harbor the greatest hope.

To the many medical professionals that have aided in my care, from head to toe, I am grateful for receiving the benefit of your knowledge, attention, and kindness. This system does not always allow for human moments, but I continue to encounter those that go above and beyond to deliver services rooted in respectful practices. To my many anonymous doners, your kindness goes beyond; thank you for this sacred trust. For these dear ones, for all the inventions, and technology, and science, I am eternally grateful.

This book has had the benefit of the love, support, and feedback of so many wonderful humans. I am lucky as an author that there is a deep sense of poetry community in the Los Angeles region that offers an open embrace to its creatives. As a voice and sound-driven poet, I have greatly appreciated rock steady poetry readings and their gracious organizers over the years, especially Cadence Collective, The Definitive Soapbox, and Two Idiots Peddling Poetry. It was here many of these poems were formed in the wake of "ooohs!," and "ahhhs.." offered in audience, or, as they happen, the awkward pauses. I am ever grateful these creatives were able to weather the displacement born from the pandemic to offer virtual readings so that our community could continue to grow together and connect with one another. A world of jazz hand clapping, little square boxes, and background photos that could make our homes look eternally clean. This strange new gathering allowed me and many disabled folx to "travel" and participate in spaces with much greater ease, and so, I count it among my blessings.

I am thrilled beyond measure to be a part of the Moon Tide family. So many of these authors have inspired with their words, and really helped me to hone in on this vision for a full book of poems. Small conversations and big with Jennifer Bradpiece, Daniel McGinn, and Ellen Webre have made their impact on me, alongside their keen friendships. Being in correspondence with Jennifer along with fellow painling and multi-modal author Tamara Hattis has helped me navigate the space between the body and the page.

Collaborations with Jessica Willson at the Los Angeles Poet Society has taught me so much about the actively forming poetry community. It has also been a joy to collaborate with Danielle Mitchell at The Poetry Lab where we geek out on poetry forms. It was there I connected with C.R. Grimmer, a kind and talented writer who has also offered encouragement and support for my writing. Poet friends Nadia the Llama, Kevin Ridgeway, and Gerard Wozek have been my creative companions and champions of the poetry life. I have been lucky to have had a wonderful teaching community of poets as well, from the offerings of Culturama and John Brantingham. Thanks also to G. Murray Thomas.

To Eric Morago, thank for the trust it takes to make books. Thank you for choosing to spend your time making this one with me. Thank you for trusting this vision. Thank you to my past editors and publishers who have been amazing to create with. To Sarah Thursday of Sadie Girl Press, especially thank you for encouraging me to include my art alongside my words. And to Alana Salts of Blanket Sea Press, thank you for recognizing the need for poetry as a means to advocate and raise awareness for the disabled community.

To my best friends Rachel Rockway and Diana Navas who have listened to me since the beginning of this journey and kept me up on the latest gossip along the way, thank you for the almost thirty years of friendship. Oh, what miracles will the next thirty bring? To all my friends, from LB Beach Clean to the folx at Stonewall, the Long Beach pals and the Santa Cruz kids, thanks for the laughs and the lessons and everything in-between.

To my parents, Wes Bryan and Terri Zwick thank you for loving me and choosing to be there for so many of those hard days. For being my hand to squeeze and second set of ears, and problem solving cohorts. I hope this book makes you a little proud of all we accomplished together.

Love and thanks to my brothers who taught me about life and chased me around with their farts just the same. I bow down to cats Basho, Issa, and Ladybug who listened to so, so, so many drafts and never complained and my sister Stacy's spirit that did the same.

A big-spooned thanks, with double scoop of ice cream and whipped cream on top to my sweet, kindhearted love, poet Robert Jay, for choosing to go on this journey with me, despite the bumpy road, and for singing Toots, Devandra, Emily and others along the way, every chance we get. And thanks of course, to you reader, for taking the time.

Also Available from Moon Tide Press

Trumpets in the Sky, Jerry Garcia (2022)

Threnody, Donna Hilbert (2022)

A Burning Lake of Paper Suns, Ellen Webre (2021)

Instructions for an Animal Body, Kelly Gray (2021)

Head *V* Heart: New & Selected Poems, Rob Sturma (2021)

*Sh!t Men Say to Me: A Poetry Anthology in Response to Toxic
    Masculinity* (2021)

Flower Grand First, Gustavo Hernandez (2021)

Everything is Radiant Between the Hates, Rich Ferguson (2020)

When the Pain Starts: Poetry as Sequential Art, Alan Passman (2020)

This Place Could Be Haunted If I Didn't Believe in Love, Lincoln
    McElwee (2020)

Impossible Thirst, Kathryn de Lancellotti (2020)

Lullabies for End Times, Jennifer Bradpiece (2020)

Crabgrass World, Robin Axworthy (2020)

Contortionist Tongue, Dania Ayah Alkhouli (2020)

The only thing that makes sense is to grow, Scott Ferry (2020)

Dead Letter Box, Terri Niccum (2019)

Tea and Subtitles: Selected Poems 1999-2019, Michael Miller (2019)

At the Table of the Unknown, Alexandra Umlas (2019)

The Book of Rabbits, Vince Trimboli (2019)

Everything I Write Is a Love Song to the World, David McIntire (2019)

Letters to the Leader, HanaLena Fennel (2019)

Darwin's Garden, Lee Rossi (2019)

Dark Ink: A Poetry Anthology Inspired by Horror (2018)

Drop and Dazzle, Peggy Dobreer (2018)

Junkie Wife, Alexis Rhone Fancher (2018)

The Moon, My Lover, My Mother, & the Dog, Daniel McGinn (2018)

Lullaby of Teeth: An Anthology of Southern California Poetry (2017)

Angels in Seven, Michael Miller (2016)

A Likely Story, Robbi Nester (2014)

Embers on the Stairs, Ruth Bavetta (2014)

The Green of Sunset, John Brantingham (2013)

The Savagery of Bone, Timothy Matthew Perez (2013)

The Silence of Doorways, Sharon Venezio (2013)

Cosmos: An Anthology of Southern California Poetry (2012)
Straws and Shadows, Irena Praitis (2012)
In the Lake of Your Bones, Peggy Dobreer (2012)
I Was Building Up to Something, Susan Davis (2011)
Hopeless Cases, Michael Kramer (2011)
One World, Gail Newman (2011)
What We Ache For, Eric Morago (2010)
Now and Then, Lee Mallory (2009)
Pop Art: An Anthology of Southern California Poetry (2009)
In the Heaven of Never Before, Carine Topal (2008)
A Wild Region, Kate Buckley (2008)
Carving in Bone: An Anthology of Orange County Poetry (2007)
Kindness from a Dark God, Ben Trigg (2007)
A Thin Strand of Lights, Ricki Mandeville (2006)
Sleepyhead Assassins, Mindy Nettifee (2006)
Tide Pools: An Anthology of Orange County Poetry (2006)
Lost American Nights: Lyrics & Poems, Michael Ubaldini (2006)

Patrons

Moon Tide Press would like to thank the following people for their support in helping publish the finest poetry from the Southern California region. To sign up as a patron, visit www.moontidepress.com or send an email to publisher@moontidepress.com.

Anonymous
Robin Axworthy
Conner Brenner
Nicole Connolly
Bill Cushing
Susan Davis
Kristen Baum DeBeasi
Peggy Dobreer
Dennis Gowans
Alexis Rhone Fancher
Hanalena Fennel
Half Off Books & Brad T. Cox
Donna Hilbert
Jim & Vicky Hoggatt
Michael Kramer
Ron Koertge & Bianca Richards
Gary Jacobelly
Ray & Christi Lacoste
Zachary & Tammy Locklin
Lincoln McElwee
David McIntire
José Enrique Medina
Michael Miller & Rachanee Srisavasdi
Michelle & Robert Miller
Ronny & Richard Morago
Terri Niccum
Andrew November
Jeremy Ra
Luke & Mia Salazar
Jennifer Smith
Andrew Turner
Rex Wilder
Mariano Zaro
Wes Bryan Zwick